Antarctica is the conti
southern end of the E
very cold, with tall mountains and deep holes. The South Pole is at the farthest south point of all.

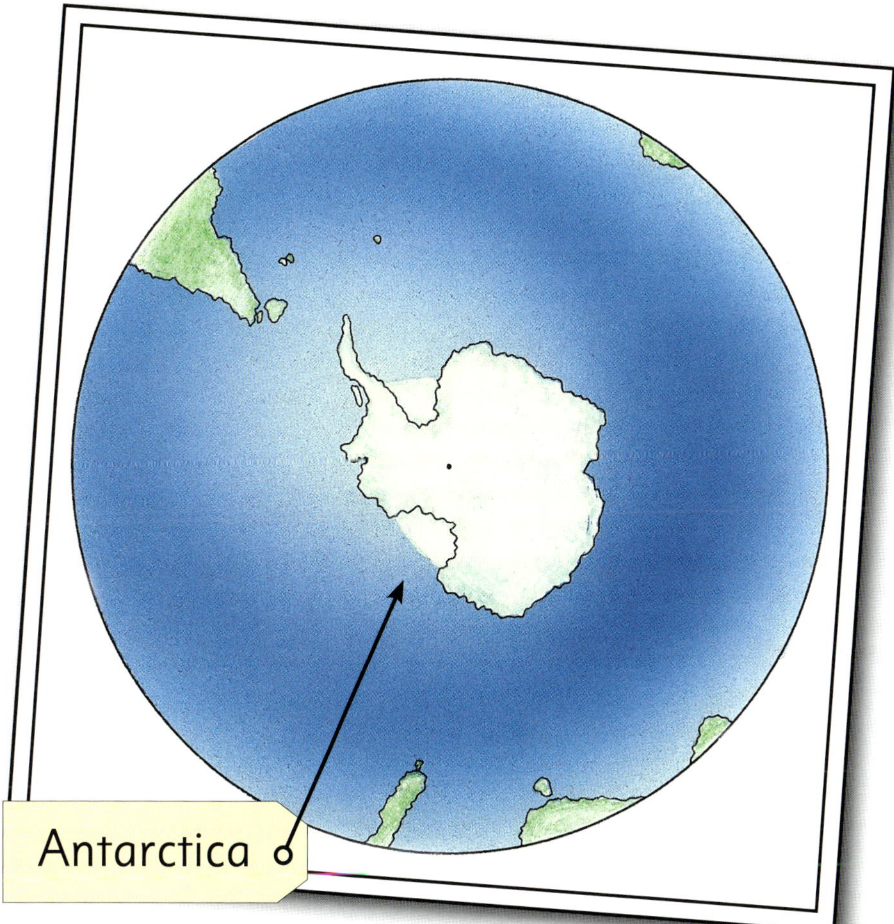

It is very hard to get to the South Pole, and in 1900 (nineteen hundred) no one had been there yet. At that time, a man called Clement Markham was planning a trip to go to Antarctica. He chose a man called Robert Scott to head the trip. Scott was a sailor and a very determined person.

On the trip, Scott and the rest of the explorers came very close to the South Pole, but they did not quite get there. They made maps of the parts of Antarctica that they had explored. When they got home, Scott was made a captain and the trip became famous.

All the same, Captain Scott was not satisfied. He was determined to go back to Antarctica and to get to the South Pole. So this time, he planned a trip to the Antarctic himself. He tried to think of everything. He had biscuits made that did not freeze in the cold!

In 1910 (nineteen ten), Captain Scott sailed for the Antarctic again. His ship was loaded with all the things that he and his explorers needed. They took little white horses and husky dogs with them on deck and they had pet rabbits hopping around too!

But things soon started to go badly. The ship was hit by bad weather. Big waves crashed down on her. The animals were kept safely inside, but some of the men's things were lost and the ship ended up with a hole in her side. They had to stop and mend the ship before they continued.

Then Captain Scott got a telegram from a man called Roald Amundsen. It said that Amundsen was headed for the South Pole too. Scott was determined to get there before him, but it was going to be hard.

When he and his men got to Antarctica, they had to sail until they found somewhere safe to land and set up camp. Then it took them just under a week to bring all the stores and equipment from the ship to the shore.

They had one big tent and lots of small ones. They set up the small ones and lived in them until they had finished building a wooden hut inside the big one. Then they lived in the hut instead.

The Antarctic can only be explored in summer, as in winter the weather is too bad. Scott and his men did not arrive until the end of the summer. This meant they had to live in the camp for a whole winter and wait until next spring before setting out for the South Pole.

food and fuel

Before setting off properly, they went ahead and left piles of food and fuel along the trail. It was going to be hard to carry all the things they needed with them, so these piles were to help them if they ran out of food and fuel on the trek back from the Pole.

It was a long, hard trek to the South Pole. They had to bring tents to sleep in as well as food, drink, and wood. The horses and dogs helped, but for much of the time the men had to drag everything themselves.

Only four men were picked to go with Scott to the Pole itself. The weather was terrible so the trip took longer than they had planned. When they got to the South Pole, they found a flag and a letter left by Amundsen, who had been there several weeks before. Scott was very disappointed.

The trek back was very, very hard and it did not go well. One man fell, hit his head, and died. The rest struggled sadly on. Then one of them, a man called Captain Oates, got very bad frostbite and had difficulty keeping up. He did not like to make everyone wait for him. One morning he left the tent, telling the rest he was just going out for a while. But he never came back.

Only three men were left. Then a very bad blizzard came down and they were trapped in the tent. They had to sit and wait for the storm to stop. But it went on for so long that they ran out of food and then out of fuel. They were starving and freezing. It was the end.

Next spring, some of the rest of the party went to look for them. They found the three men still in the tent. They had written letters about the trek and what had happened to them.

At present, the continent of Antarctica is protected. There is a base there, where researchers from all different lands can go to help study the Antarctic. It is called the Scott-Amundsen base.